FRUITS and VEGETABLES

by Rebecca Phillips-Bartlett

Minneapolis, Minnesota

Credits
All images are courtesy of Shutterstock.com, unless otherwise specified. With thanks to Getty Images, Thinkstock Photo, and iStockphoto. Recurring - Markus Mainka, Ruslan__Grebeshkov. Cover - grey_and, Serg64. 4-5 - New Africa, monticello. 6-7 - Roman Samokhin, Kovaleva_Ka, Superheang168, Boonchuay1970, Nataly Studio. 8-9 - Pavle Bugarski, KarepaStock, yuris, barmalini. 10-11 - Brian Mueller, Romolo Tavani, kuvona, mahirart, itor. 12-13 - Brendan Delany, kukuruxa, Paul Maguire, tchara. 14-15 - Annaev, nednapa. 16-17 - Rudmer Zwerver, Viktor Loki. 18-19 - Africa Studio, Prostock-studio. 20-21 - Tim UR, Sergiy Akhundov, Nataly Studio. 22-23 - TierneyMJ, Pressmaster.

Bearport Publishing Company Product Development Team
President: Jen Jenson; Director of Product Development: Spencer Brinker; Managing Editor: Allison Juda; Associate Editor: Naomi Reich; Associate Editor: Tiana Tran; Art Director: Colin O'Dea; Designer: Kim Jones; Designer: Kayla Eggert; Product Development Assistant: Owen Hamlin

Library of Congress Cataloging-in-Publication Data is available at www.loc.gov or upon request from the publisher.

ISBN: 979-8-88916-952-9 (hardcover)
ISBN: 979-8-88916-956-7 (paperback)
ISBN: 979-8-89232-129-7 (ebook)

© 2025 BookLife Publishing
This edition is published by arrangement with BookLife Publishing.

North American adaptations © 2025 Bearport Publishing Company. All rights reserved. No part of this publication may be reproduced in whole or in part, stored in any retrieval system, or transmitted in any form or by any means, electronic, mechanical, photocopying, recording, or otherwise, without written permission from the publisher. Bearport Publishing is a division of Chrysalis Education Group.

For more information, write to Bearport Publishing, 5357 Penn Avenue South, Minneapolis, MN 55419.

CONTENTS

Plenty of Plants 4
Fantastic Fruits and Vegetables . . . 5
Fruit Features 6
Vegetable Varieties 8
Surprising Fruits 10
Where They Grow. 12
Amazing for Animals 16
Perfect for People. 18
Identifying Fruits and Veggies 20
Finding Fruits and Veggies 22
Glossary. 24
Index 24

PLENTY OF PLANTS

Our world is full of amazing plants. Humans and animals use these plants in lots of different ways.

Let's explore this *plant-iful* world all around us!

PLANTS CAN GROW IN THE GROUND, IN WATER, OR ON OTHER THINGS.

FANTASTIC FRUITS AND VEGETABLES

What are fruits and vegetables? These are the parts of plants that we eat. There are many kinds of fruits and veggies.

WHAT ARE YOUR FAVORITE FRUITS AND VEGGIES?

FRUIT FEATURES

Many fruits look and taste very different from one another. However, there are some things that all fruits have in common.

SEEDS

All fruits have seeds. Some, such as peaches, have one large seed called a stone. Other fruits have many small seeds.

SOME KINDS OF BANANAS HAVE TINY, BLACK SEEDS.

SKIN

Fruits are covered with skins that **protect** their seeds from harm. Some skins are **edible**, which means they can be eaten. Other skins taste bad or are too hard to eat.

KIWIS HAVE BROWN, FURRY SKIN.

APPLES HAVE THIN, SHINY SKIN.

WHICH FRUITS DO YOU PEEL BEFORE EATING?

VEGETABLE VARIETIES

Vegetables are other parts of plants that we eat. There are many kinds of veggies.

LEAVES

We eat the leaves of some plants, such as lettuce and spinach.

Lettuce leaf

ROOTS AND BULBS

The edible parts of some plants grow underground. Carrots and beets are roots. Onions and garlic are **bulbs**.

A carrot

An onion

STEMS AND FLOWERS

Other veggies, such as celery, are a plant's stem. And the part of broccoli that most people eat is actually a flower.

Celery

Broccoli

SURPRISING FRUITS

Sometimes, it can be hard to tell if something is a fruit or a vegetable. People often think of fruits as being only sweet. However, many foods that people think are veggies are actually fruits because they have seeds.

AVOCADOS, PUMPKINS, PEPPERS, TOMATOES, AND CUCUMBERS ARE ALL FRUITS.

NUTS

Some nuts are also fruits! A nut is a hard-shelled fruit with a seed inside. Chestnuts, hazelnuts, and pecans are all fruits.

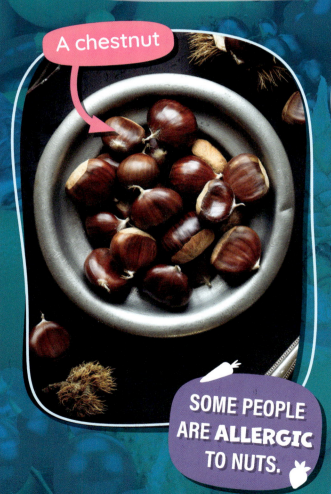

A chestnut

A hazelnut

A pecan

SOME PEOPLE ARE ALLERGIC TO NUTS.

WHERE THEY GROW

Many types of plants have fruits and vegetables. They grow in different ways.

TREES AND BUSHES

Apples, oranges, and peaches are some of the fruits that grow on trees. Other fruits, such as blueberries, grow on bushes.

An orange tree

A blueberry bush

VINES

Some fruits grow on **vines**. Vines with large fruits, such as melons and pumpkins, grow along the ground. The vines with smaller fruits may climb up trees, rocks, or other things.

Melon vine

Tomato vine

PEOPLE USE STICKS OR CAGES TO HOLD UP TOMATO VINES.

GROWING UNDERGROUND

It can be hard to know when it's time to pick vegetables that grow underground. Many root veggies, such as carrots, start to poke out of the dirt when they are ready.

Carrots

Parsnips and potatoes give other clues for when their underground vegetables are ready. Their leaves above ground sag and often turn yellow when it is time to **harvest**.

A potato

AMAZING FOR ANIMALS

Wild animals have to find their own food. Those that eat only plants are called **herbivores** (HUR-buh-vorz). They often munch on fruits and veggies.

When animals eat fruits, the seeds pass through their bodies and come out in their poop. This helps spread the seeds to new places where they can grow into more plants.

PERFECT FOR PEOPLE

Fruits and veggies are healthy to eat! Some taste great when eaten raw. Others are better when cooked. These foods are full of **nutrients** that help keep our bodies working well.

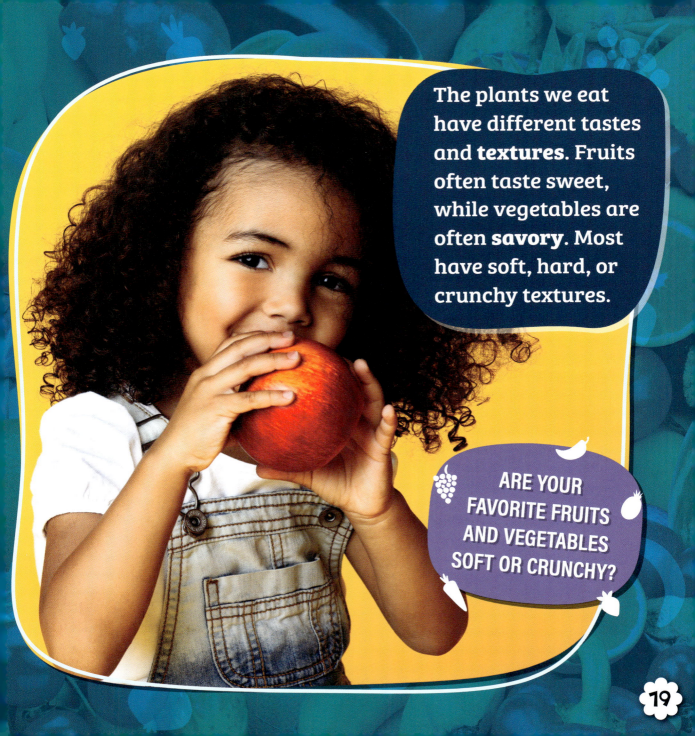

The plants we eat have different tastes and **textures**. Fruits often taste sweet, while vegetables are often **savory**. Most have soft, hard, or crunchy textures.

ARE YOUR FAVORITE FRUITS AND VEGETABLES SOFT OR CRUNCHY?

IDENTIFYING FRUITS AND VEGGIES

There are many different fruits and vegetables. Can you match the descriptions below to the pictures on page 21?

1. Passion fruit has purple skin and lots of small seeds inside.

2. Walnuts are fruits with hard, tan shells.

3. We eat the stems of rhubarb plants. They are long and red.

Answers: 1) Passion fruit is C. 2) Walnuts are A. 3) Rhubarb is B.

21

FINDING FRUITS AND VEGGIES

There are many kinds of fruits and vegetables you could try. You might buy them at grocery stores or grow them in a garden. Do you know which of the foods you eat are fruits and which are vegetables?

Next time you go outside, look at the plants near you. Do any of them have fruits or vegetables? Write down what you see. There are plenty of plants to explore!

SOME PLANTS CAN MAKE YOU SICK. ALWAYS ASK A GROWN-UP BEFORE PICKING PLANTS.

GLOSSARY

allergic having a bad reaction to something

bulbs rounded, underground parts of some plants from which the rest of the plant grows

edible able to be eaten

harvest to pick or gather plants that are ready to be eaten

herbivores animals that eat only plants

nutrients substances needed by plants and animals to grow and stay healthy

protect to keep something safe

savory a taste that is spicy or salty

textures how things feel when touched

vines plants with long stems that grow along the ground or climb on other things for support

INDEX

bulbs 9
bushes 12
flowers 9
leaves 8, 15
nuts 11, 20

poop 17
roots 9, 14
seeds 6-7, 10-11, 17, 20

skin 7, 20
stems 9, 20
trees 12-13
vines 13